T0009041

POCKET BUILDER
VEHICLES

WRITTEN BY
TORI KOSARA

INTRODUCTION

This book is packed with ideas and tricks to help you become a better LEGO® builder, whether you're building with LEGO bricks for the first or the thousandth time. Start with the handy building tips on page 4, then grab your LEGO collection, choose a page, and get moving! With advice and building techniques for making things that go, you'll be a LEGO building expert in no time. What will you make?

Find me on page 70!

Chapter 3: Sky

Chapter 4: Space

It's time to build!

Let's get a move on!

BUILDING TIPS

Are you ready to start thinking like a LEGO® builder? Try some of these ideas or come up with your own way of doing things. Whatever you do, just remember to have fun!

GETTING STARTED

There's one thing you'll definitely need before you can build: LEGO pieces! Don't worry about the size of your collection or how new it is. The original LEGO® System in Play elements (made from 1958) fit perfectly with those made today. You can also buy second-hand LEGO pieces at thrift stores, share with friends and neighbors, or play with them at schools and libraries.

There's a whole raft of helpful tips!

SCALE UP OR DOWN

Decide what scale you want your model to be before you start. That way, you will have the right number of LEGO pieces ready.

SORT YOUR BRICKS

Organize your collection into element types and colors to save time as you build.

FIND A BUILDING SPACE

Look for a flat surface with plenty of room for building and storing your pieces, such as a table.

SWAP IT OUT

If you don't have the perfect piece, think about other parts you can use instead.

BUILD TOGETHER

Ask a family member or a friend to join in and share the joy of building. You might learn new things from each other or give each other new ideas!

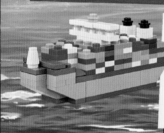

CHOOSE YOUR COLORS

Use whatever colors you like when you're building. Your vehicles can look however you want!

DON'T PANIC!

There is no right or wrong way to build. If your model doesn't turn out how you wanted it to, rebuild it or try something new.

KEEP BUILDING

The fun is in the building, so just keep connecting your bricks until things click for you.

CHAPTER 1
LAND

ICE-CREAM TRUCK

Avoid model-making meltdowns by building the ice-cream truck's body and roof separately. This way, you can fill up your freezer and add finishing touches before you connect the top.

Now that's what I call cool!

Curved slopes attach to 1×4 tiles with studs

Studs on the serving window let you attach frozen treats

BRIGHT IDEA

Two plates with pin holes keep the transparent tile "headlights" secure on either side of the hood.

1×2 plate with pin hole

LEGO® Technic half pin

1×1 transparent round tile

GINGERBREAD CAR

When it comes to creativity, this vehicle takes the cake! Brown bricks and printed tiles make a sweet ride fit for a gingerbread person. What pieces will you use to cook up a fantasy food car?

BUILD TIP!

Just like when you bake cookies, make the model first and add the decorations at the end.

White tiles look like smooth icing

Glittery round tile for a sweet-looking door handle

KEY INGREDIENT

This car can't go anywhere without a sturdy base. Use any color bricks to form the chassis, then build upward.

1×2/2×4 bracket ....

.... Stack of 2×6 plates

1×4 tile ....

ALL-TERRAIN VEHICLE (ATV)

When it comes to building vehicles, think about the types of surfaces you'll be rolling over. An ATV like this one needs chunky tires so it can tackle tough terrain.

I'm ready to roll!

Stacks of gray plates form a sturdy base

Plate with bar handle is a step for minifigures to climb aboard

3×4 plate with mudguard

1×1 round plates

KEEP IT UP

Stacks of 1×1 round plates raise the mudguards so that these big wheels have plenty of space to spin.

Large wheel with tire

MOTORCYCLE AND SIDECAR

You could zip off on solo adventures with a motorcycle. But like building, road trips are more fun with a friend! Design a simple passenger sidecar like this one, which is made mainly by stacking plates. Connect it to a motorcycle model for double the fun.

Spare tire attaches to a jumper plate

Move aside! We're coming through.

The sidecar has only one wheel

PUT A PIN IN IT

Two LEGO Technic axle pins fit into a LEGO Technic beam that links the sidecar to the motorcycle.

LEGO Technic axle pin

LEGO Technic beam

FARM TRACTOR

Yippee-i-e-i-o! It's easy to make a hard-working tractor to help your minifigures with all those tough farm chores. Start by building the engine and cab, then add the wheels.

BUILD TIP!

Use plates to attach the underside of the vehicle's body to the wheels below.

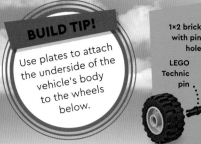

1×2 brick with pin hole

LEGO Technic pin

2×2 plate with pins

A WHEEL CONNECTION

These wheels are attached using two different types of pin connections. Use whatever LEGO Technic pins you have.

Transparent pieces for good visibility from the cab

Plates form steps so the driver can reach the cab

"Hay"—nice ride!

PICKUP TRUCK

This pickup truck is built in the same way as many vehicle models—from the bottom up. It has a big open flatbed at the back so that your minifigures can add all the tools, accessories, or camping gear they need to get rolling.

BUILD TIP!

Make sure your roof has studs so you can connect more equipment if needed.

4×4x$^2/_3$ wedges top the hood and the roof

Panels keep cargo stored safely in the bed

1×2 grille tiles look like a large grille

SIDE ON

Rows of bricks with side studs on both sides of the build let you attach plates and curved slopes to make doors.

2×2 curved slope

2×4 plate connects curved slopes to the bricks with side studs

CEMENT MIXER

The cement mixer's drum rests on top of a sturdy base of plates. Why not mix things up and swap out the drum for other equipment, such as a skip or a jackhammer arm? There are loads of ways to build and rebuild!

Two 3×3×2 cones connect to make the drum

What should we build today?

Ingot piece looks like the truck's electric system

Any transparent 1×1 tiles can form headlights

3×3×2 cone

LEGO Technic cross axle

LEGO Technic cross block

DRUM STICK

A LEGO Technic cross axle slides through the drum to secure it. The axle fits into a LEGO Technic cross block to hold it at an angle.

CRAWLER CRANE

Level up your models by building in parts that add movement to your creations. One plate with a bar fits into a plate with a clip. This lets the crawler crane's boom tilt up and down just like a real crane's.

If you don't have LEGO® string, attach your "hook" to a stud on the boom instead

BUILD TIP!

Make sure the boom isn't too tall so that your crane build doesn't topple over.

Stack plates and slopes to make the tracks

1×2 plate fits into a plate with clip

TURN IT

If you want your cab to rotate from side to side, connect the bottom of the cab to a 2×2 turntable piece.

2×2 turntable piece ......

...... 4×4 plate

MONSTER TRUCK RALLY

This monster truck racetrack is built on two 16×16 baseplates, but you could make yours as big or as small as you like. Add in a track, obstacles, and stands so your fans can watch the action!

ON THE SIDE

Connect curved arch pieces on their sides to create hoops for your monster trucks to "jump" through!

LEGO Technic half pin

1×1 headlight brick

1×3×2 curved brick

Use transparent flame pieces for obstacles

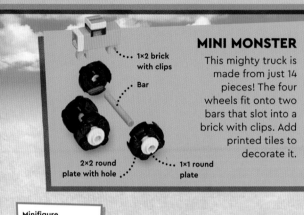

MINI MONSTER

This mighty truck is made from just 14 pieces! The four wheels fit onto two bars that slot into a brick with clips. Add printed tiles to decorate it.

1×2 brick with clips

Bar

2×2 round plate with hole

1×1 round plate

Minifigure statuettes fill the stadium stands

Use curved and straight tiles for the track

Slope bricks create hills for the trucks to climb

This build is a real winner!

ELEVATED TRAIN

Level up and make an elevated railroad track for trains. Use plates to steady the brick-built columns that support your track. Then add rows of bricks to connect the columns. Top them with two rows of plates and tiles to make smooth tracks.

Round plate "wheels" glide along the plate and tile tracks

Inverted dome makes a funnel

2×6 plate determines the width of the build

This build is right on track!

Stacks of bricks connect each section of track

Wheels attach sideways

FULL STEAM AHEAD

What's a track without a train? Make sure the base of your train is the right width to fit along your elevated track.

MINING CART

Before the invention of the engine, many vehicles, like this mining cart, were pulled by horses. Build the part of the model that attaches to the horse first to be sure that the vehicle is at the right height so its wheels can roll along.

Horse hitching piece connects the horse and cart

Brown pieces for an old-fashioned wooden look

This build is all mine!

1×2 plate with bar

SIDE ANGLE

Plates with bars and plates with clips keep two sides of the cart at an angle. The hinge connection lets you open the sides for easier loading.

1×2 plate with clip

CITY BUS

Beep, beep! Minifigures will love a bus ride around town. Use transparent pieces like the panels on this bus so that every passenger gets a pretty city view!

Tile makes a destination sign

1×2×2 transparent panels make good bus windows

Next stop, Brickston!

1×1 transparent round plate makes an indicator light

ON TOP

The roof is built on plates, which can easily be removed so that you can access the inside of the model.

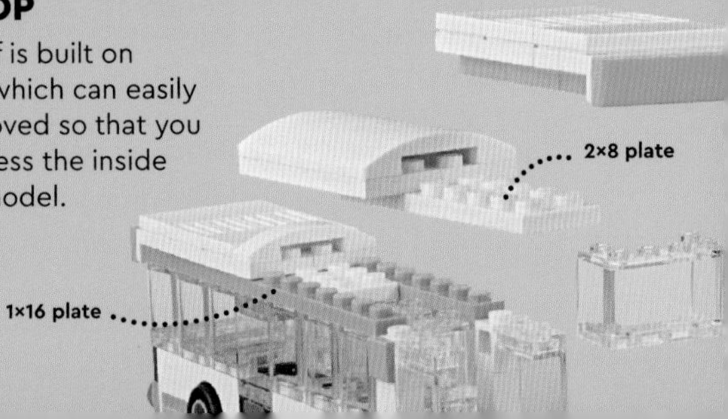

2×8 plate

1×16 plate

AUTO RICKSHAW

Have you noticed anything unusual about this cool city passenger vehicle? It has only three wheels! The key to a three-wheeled build is to make the single wheel at the front level with the wheels at the back. Then it can zip through urban streets!

BUILD TIP!

Build the front and back walls higher than three bricks so that your minifigures fit.

2×2 plate with single wheel holder

1×1 plate with ring looks like a side mirror

Bar slots into 1×1 round plates with holes to form a handrail

RIDE INSIDE

Make room for your minifigures by adding a driver's seat piece and a 2×2 plate at the back for your passenger to sit on.

Handlebars for steering

2×2 plate makes a passenger seat

Driver's seat

DRAG RACER

For maximum racing speed, a dragster needs a narrow lightweight chassis. Use a long plate like the one here for the base and add curved slopes for a streamlined hood.

This race is a real drag!

Smooth tires help race cars reach higher speeds

1×6 curved slopes reduce drag to make the car go faster

SPOILED

The piece at the back is called a spoiler. Use a hinge plate and brick to angle yours so that the force of the wind keeps the car on the track.

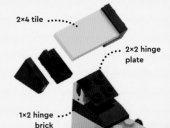

2×4 tile

2×2 hinge plate

1×2 hinge brick

BUILD TIP!

Race cars are all about speed. Use just enough pieces to keep your model lightweight.

SPORTS CAR

Quick-moving sports cars like this one are built low to the ground so that they can handle tight turns. To get a sporty look like this, build only a few bricks upward from the chassis. And don't forget racing stripes to complete the look!

BUILD TIP!

This car is built on a chassis piece. If you don't have one, use plates instead.

I wheely want to drive that!

3×4×1 windshield is angled for a sleek, sporty look

Two 3×2 slopes support the roof

REAR VIEW

Remove the roof tiles to transform the car into a convertible! Replace the slope at the back with one of the tiles so it appears folded.

1×4 tile

2×4 tile

Find this cool powerboat on page 36.

CHAPTER 2
SEA

DEEP SEA SUB

Explore beyond the shore with a deep sea submersible model like this one. Use ball and socket joints to connect movable "robotic" arms so that your minifigures can search for treasure.

BUILD TIP!

Make sure the driver's seat has studs to keep the minifigure in place.

Plate with socket connects the arm to a plate with ball joint on the sub

I wonder what I'll see in the sea . . .

6×3×3 domed windshield makes a cockpit window

1×3×2 curved arch

1×1 round plates light the way

SHAPE UP

Eight curved arches form the roof and top of the sub's walls. The arches give the submersible a recognizable shape and leave plenty of room for the sub driver's head.

Pilot sits on this plate

AMPHIBIOUS CAR

This car was built to speed around over ground *and* underwater! Make a watertight vehicle with large cockpit windows, such as these windshields. Remove them to create a convertible when your minifigures are driving on land.

Nothing fishy about this car!

6×6×3 domed windshield to keep the driver dry

Flippers create a nautical car door handle

MOVING ON

A propeller piece attaches to a 2×2 plate with pin at the back of the vehicle to help it move through the water.

Propeller piece

2×2 plate with pin

PIRATE SHIP

Ahoy, matey! To make a pirate ship's shape, you'll need a flat-bottomed hull with sloping sides. Small slope bricks make angled walls when they're attached to a double inverted slope like this one.

> *Make a splash with any colors you like!*

6×4×²⁄₃ curved wedge plate makes a sail

HOIST THE SAIL

A tall bar piece raises the sail so that it's high enough to give the captain space and catch the strong sea breezes.

Double inverted slope forms the hull's base

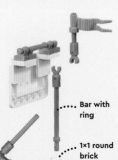

.... Bar with ring

.... 1×1 round brick

BUILD TIP!

How many buccaneers will fit in your ship? Make sure there is room for everyone!

GHOST SHIP

A boat to keep spirits afloat is scarily fun to build! Build your zombie pirate crew a sturdy ship. Then add plenty of ghostly details, such as bones, jack-o'-lanterns, and anything else they need as they set sail for a treasure haunt.

Rows of bones and tail pieces make tattered sails

Hey! Where are you going?

Robot arms clip to pieces with bars to look like bones

HAUNTED HOUSE

Stacks of standard and slope bricks create creepy crew quarters at the back of the ship.

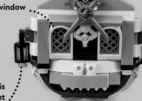

Lattice window

1×1 round brick is an eerie light

AIR-CUSHION VEHICLE (ACV)

Panel pieces make sturdy walls around the driver of this air-cushion vehicle (ACV). With a wide, smooth base known as a skirt, the ACV can glide over both land and water.

Spinning propeller is a tile attached to a 2×2 turntable

This skirt really floats my boat!

1×1 corner panel forms part of the side and front wall

PUT ON A SKIRT

The sides of the skirt attach to bricks with side studs. Use curved pieces on each corner to give the skirt its rounded shape.

1×1 brick with side stud

1×2×1⅓ curved brick

4×4 plate is the base

SWAMP AIRBOAT

Airboats like this one need long, flat bottoms for skimming over shallow waters, such as swamps. Use plates of any size to form the base, then build upward. The sides of this boat are made with slopes and panel pieces.

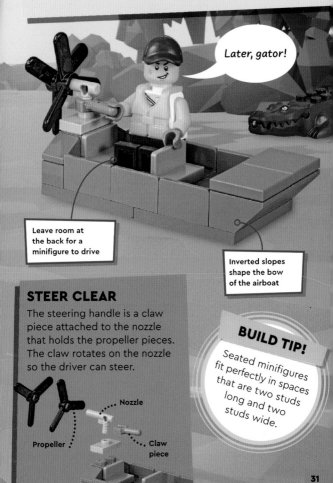

Later, gator!

Leave room at the back for a minifigure to drive

Inverted slopes shape the bow of the airboat

STEER CLEAR

The steering handle is a claw piece attached to the nozzle that holds the propeller pieces. The claw rotates on the nozzle so the driver can steer.

Nozzle

Propeller

Claw piece

BUILD TIP!

Seated minifigures fit perfectly in spaces that are two studs long and two studs wide.

CONTAINER SHIP

This impressive freight-filled ship is made mostly by stacking standard pieces. Long bricks form the side walls, which are topped with a large plate. Then the bridge and cargo are built on top.

1×1 round plate on two 1×1 plates looks like a chimney

Which container are the snacks in?

3×1 slopes on either side of the hull form the bow

2×6 brick attaches to plates above and below it

PLATE UP

The ship's containers are stacks of plates in different sizes and colors. They attach to the plate that makes up the ship's deck.

1×2 plate

1×4 plate

VIKING LONGSHIP

A Viking longship should be longer than it is wide, but make sure there is room for your Viking crew to fit on board! Brown bricks give the ship an authentic look, but you can use any colors you have.

The sea serpent's head is built on two 1×3×2 curved arches

SET SAIL

This patterned sail is made from a row of 2×8 plates. Wedge pieces at the ends make it look as though it's billowing in the wind.

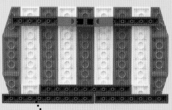

Brown plates hold the sail's stripes together

That ship reminds me of someone . . .

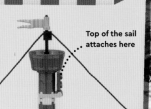

Top of the sail attaches here

CRUISE SHIP

Cruise ships can carry thousands of vacationers, so be sure to build in room for plenty of travelers! Stacks of 1×2 grille tiles form the passenger decks. The grooves in the plates look like windows for the ship's guest cabins.

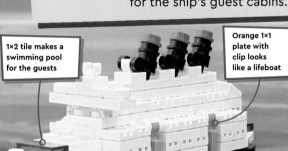

1×2 tile makes a swimming pool for the guests

Orange 1×1 plate with clip looks like a lifeboat

BUILD TIP!

Take it one piece at a time. Build the hull first, then add the upper decks.

That ship is jaw-some!

LET'S SPLIT

Each side of the hull is made of curved pieces. They connect to a row of bricks with side studs in the center of the ship.

1×2 curved slope

1×2 brick with side studs

LEGO® string with studs looks like sail rigging

I said "row," not "slow"!

Torches fit into plates with clips to light the way

The boat should be wider in the middle

BUILD TIP!

To add shields to the sides, build bricks with side studs into the ship's walls.

SPEEDY POWERBOAT

Shape is key to making a boat that can really zip along! Curved pieces make for a streamlined craft that easily cuts through air and water. Don't forget to add a powerful engine at the back of the boat to keep things moving.

Wave goodbye!

Keep your minifigures safe with a life jacket and helmet

BUILD TIP!

Build in enough space for one driver so your craft isn't weighed down by gear or passengers.

Hose nozzle engine controls fit into pieces with clips

6×4 inverted wedge forms a streamlined hull

SLIDE ON

A 2×2 slide plate on the underside of the boat's hull gives it extra stability so it can zoom around at high speeds!

6×4 curved angle slope

2×6 plate

6×4 double inverted slope

2×2 slide plate

ONE-PERSON KAYAK

This cool kayak for one has a simple design so your minifigures will be paddling off on adventures in no time! The base is a narrow plate with slopes at either end. Cover most of the studs with tiles for a sleek, waterproof look.

Safely store supplies on a 2×2 round plate

Bowline for docking is a string with two studs

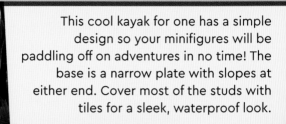

Inverted slope forms the kayak's bow shape

Is there room for me?

HAVE A WALL

The kayak's side walls are tiles that fit onto bricks with side studs. Add more plates and bricks with side studs to make a longer kayak.

1×1 brick with side stud

1×6 tile

RESCUE BOAT

Need an inflatable look for your lifeboat model? 2×2 round bricks to the rescue! These pieces create plump, curved sides that make this search and rescue raft look like it can really float on the water.

I'm on my way!

Steering console connects to a brick with side studs in the base

Stacks of 2×2 round bricks form the sides

Two small slopes look like space for anchor stowage

THIS SIDE UP

The base is built sideways. You could stack pieces upward, then turn the model on its side before adding the steering wheel and emergency light.

Bow and stern attach to two rows of round bricks

Bow is mainly made of slopes

FERRY BOAT

Ferries shuttle cars, trucks, and passengers across the water. Create a wide deck with a 4×8 plate to park your micro vehicles on. The plate's studs hold the cars and trucks in place no matter how bumpy the ride.

Upside-down 1×1 bucket handle looks like radio antennas

We are "ferry" close to shore!

Passenger cars are made from jumper plates and tiles

Plate with bar ramp hinges up and down

RAIL SAFE

1×2 plates with handles attach sideways to a row of bracket plates on either side of the hull to create safety rails for the passenger cars.

1×2/2×2 bracket plate

1×2 plate with handle

TWO-PERSON ROWBOAT

Make everything shipshape by using slope pieces to form the side walls of your rowboat. These pieces give the craft a classic curved shape and an instantly seaworthy look so that your minifigures can merrily row along.

Steer clear of that giant fish!

Oars lock into 1×1 plates with clips

LEGO string with studs connects the wakeboarder to the boat

Flotation ring fits onto a 1×2 jumper plate on the bow

Curved pieces fit onto bricks with side studs

2×2 corner plate

8×1 curved slope

GET IT CORNERED

Attach two 2×2 corner plates at the center of each 8×1 curved slope. This way, you can add a smaller slope below the 8×1 slope to close up any gaps in the hull.

RACING PLANES

Take to the skies by building small, fast planes and challenge your friends to a race. You could even time yourselves to find out who can build a plane in the fastest time. Get ready for liftoff!

Wings are stacks of bricks connected to the plane sideways

Small stack of slopes forms the tail fin

1×1 round plates and cones make landing skids

IN A SPIN

A bar fits through the propeller to join it to the nose of the plane, which is made from a 2×2×2 cone.

Propeller

1×1 round plate with hole

Bar

2×2×2 cone connects to 2×2 round plate with axle hole

EGYPTIAN SKIFF

Build like an Ancient Egyptian and create a traditional skiff. You could make just one boat. Or why not build two identical designs and connect them with a 10×10 rope net? It looks just like those used for catching fish on the River Nile.

Row, row, row your skiff . . .

Tan pieces look like the papyrus these ancient vessels were made from

1×1 round plate with leaf attaches to side studs

10×10 rope net loops onto 1×1 round bricks

This boat is ancient hiss-tory!

Sternpost is decorated with leaves

Inverted arch gives the stempost height

HIGH SIDE

Use inverted arch bricks to create tall stemposts and sternposts. Then add your own decorations so your boat is easy to identify at sea.

CHAPTER 3
SKY

HOVERING HELICOPTER

Some helicopters, like this one, have no closing doors! Build the body of the 'copter on a plate by stacking bricks and slopes. Be sure to leave a gap for your minifigure pilot to enter and exit.

Two different-sized plates form the roof

Want to go for a spin?

A stack of two slopes and one brick look like a tail fin

Long plates or minifigure skis make good landing skids

GOING UP!

Ready for takeoff? Two 1×10 plates look like rotor blades. They can really spin thanks to a 2×2 turntable piece.

······· 1×10 plate

2×2 jumper plate ·······

2×2 turntable

BUILD TIP!

Before you complete the build, test the width of your doorway to make sure your minifigures can fit.

WING IT

Bracket plates at the center of this plane allow the wings to connect. Make the wings identical so that your minifigures have a smooth ride.

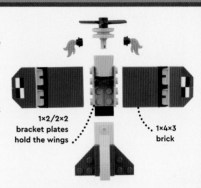

1×2/2×2 bracket plates hold the wings

1×4×3 brick

It's "plane" sailing up here!

Four plates make a checkered pattern

2×2 wedge plate for a streamlined tail design

BUILD TIP!

No pieces with side studs? You could build wings from long plates that stretch across a plane's fuselage (body).

Wingtips move up and down on hinge plates

EARLY AIRPLANE

Old-fashioned planes look more like gliders than modern jets. Build in two sets of wings to create an extra-sturdy airplane for your minifigures as they fly back in time.

BUILD TIP!

Use sturdy pieces like telescopes to separate your wings so that they won't collapse during flight.

1×2 plate with clip holds a bar to secure the front of the plane

Tan 2×10 plate looks like the cloth the wings would have been made of

Telescope pieces are struts

Horse hitching piece

Sorry. There's only room for one!

LEVEL UP
Start with the lower horse harness and build the bottom level to create a stable base before building upward.

ULTRALIGHT TRIKE

Build an ultralight aircraft so that your minifigures can glide in style! Use angle or wedge plates to shape the wings, which are known as airfoils. The design of the wings help catch the currents that keep the glider flying through the air.

4×4 wedge plates on both sides for an angled shape

Stack 1×1 round bricks to make rigging

All clear for landing!

Wheels roll for takeoff and landing

GET AROUND

Propellers help push these little vehicles through the air. This propeller piece rotates around a 1×2 brick with pin.

Propeller

1×2 brick with pin

HOT-AIR BALLOON

Don't go in circles! Building a round envelope (balloon) is a breeze. Stack bricks from the bottom up, making each layer a little wider than the one below it. After you reach the middle, make the layers above narrower.

The widest layer of the balloon should be the middle

This is really uplifting!

Tall bricks link the envelope to the basket below

1×6 arch

6×6 plate

BASKET OF BRICKS

Give your minifigure a gondola (basket) to ride in. 1×6 arches around the edges of a 6×6 plate form the gondola's sides.

BUILD TIP!

Take care not to make the envelope too big. Otherwise, your model will not be stable.

HIGH-FLYING JETPACK

Soar into the future and build small-but-mighty personal flyers with just a handful of little pieces. Just be sure not to make the jetpacks too bulky or your minifigures won't be able to take to the skies.

> *Why walk when you can fly?*

Personalize your flyer with printed tiles

1×2 brick with side studs

Neck bracket

1×3 robot arm with open stud for pilot controls

T-bar

BRACE YOURSELF

To design a jetpack, stack small pieces onto a neck bracket. It fits between the minifigure's head and shoulders.

BUILD TIP!

Secure the neck bracket to the minifigure. Then build the jetpack upward and outward.

DRONE (UAV)

Minifigures can't ride on drones (also called unmanned aerial vehicles, or UAVs), but they can take them for a spin! You'll need to build a remote control as well as the UAV so that you can pretend your minifigures are driving from the ground.

Your drone could have as many propellers as you like

I think I've got the hang of this!

Jumper plate makes a camera to film land below

Remote control base is a 1×2 plate with handles

LEGO® Technic pin connector with clips

JUMP UP

Center the drone's propeller section on a base made from a 1×2 jumper plate like this one so it flies along evenly.

1×2 jumper plate

1×1 transparent round title for a spinning propeller

51

SOARING TAXI

This special cab doesn't drive around on wheels. Instead, it has wings so passengers can sail over traffic and zip around town. If you want your taxi to have a roof, build up the sides and top them with plates.

The body of the taxi looks like a car

6×8 curved hull plate for smooth landings

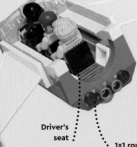

MAKE A SEAT

Hold your driver and passengers securely in place with driver's seats.

Driver's seat

1×1 round tile makes a taillight

I'll parachute out right there, please!

BUILD TIP!

Find your wing pieces first so you can think about how and where to attach them.

Large tail fin is usually used on the back of planes

Customize your vehicle with colorful tiles on the wingtips

FLIGHT CONNECTION

A row of four bracket plates on either side of the vehicle holds the wings in place.

1×2/2×2 bracket plate

FLYING CAR

This model looks as if it's flown in from the future, but it's a blast from the past! Just like this micro model, 1950s flying cars had plastic bodies and removable wings. They weren't quite as easy to build, though!

Tail fin is built on a plate with bar that clips to the back

Should we drive or fly there?

Detach the 4×2 wedge plate wings to convert to car mode

Just two plates make up the body of the car

PIN WHEELS

All four wheels are 1×1 round tiles. They fit onto LEGO Technic half pins, which slide through two 2×2 plates with rings.

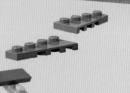

LEGO Technic half pin

2×2 plate with rings

1×1 round tile

SMALL SEAPLANE

Two 6×1 inverted curved slopes attached to the bottom of this plane make floats that let the plane land on and take off from a watery "runway." To transform the aircraft into a terrestrial plane, swap the slopes for wheel pieces instead.

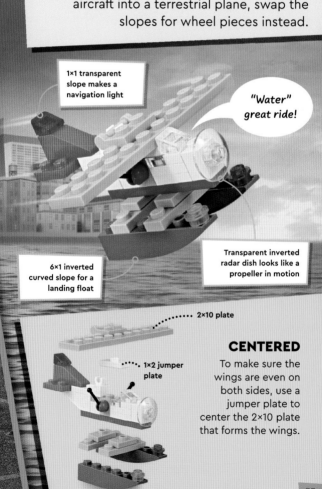

1×1 transparent slope makes a navigation light

"Water" great ride!

6×1 inverted curved slope for a landing float

Transparent inverted radar dish looks like a propeller in motion

2×10 plate

1×2 jumper plate

CENTERED

To make sure the wings are even on both sides, use a jumper plate to center the 2×10 plate that forms the wings.

POLICE PLANE

Police planes help support the force on the ground. With a large cockpit window and plenty of high-tech gadgets, this plane is ready to help on search and rescue missions at sea.

Two wedge plates make stabilizers

8×4×2 windshield with handle fits into a clip so it can open

Give me a wave! Over.

Use a boat hull piece for a sturdy base

IN CONTROL

Give your police pilot all the tools they need, including a joystick for steering and printed tiles with controls to help on their missions.

Joystick

1×2 printed tile control panel

STUNT AIRPLANE

Build a plane just for fun! Loop de loop, roll, and race around the course in a colorful stunt plane made for doing tricks. Why not level up the fun with unexpected details, such as cupcake pieces on the wings?

These unusual landing lights are cupcake pieces

BUILD TIP!

Get creative with colors and details to make a plane that shows off your fun side.

2×2 transparent slope makes a cockpit window

Leave the cockpit open or add walls and a roof

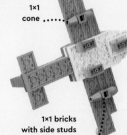

1×1 cone

LOOK OUT BELOW

There are more details on the underside! The two engines are made of a sideways stack of a 1×1 cone, 1×1 brick with side studs, and 1×1 round brick.

1×1 bricks with side studs connect the engines to the wings

CLOUD CAR

Head in the clouds? Then you're ready to build a fantastic fantasy vehicle like this self-driving cloud car. There's room for a passenger, or it can simply drive itself across the sky painting rainbows.

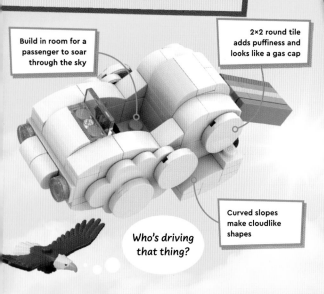

Build in room for a passenger to soar through the sky

2×2 round tile adds puffiness and looks like a gas cap

Curved slopes make cloudlike shapes

Who's driving that thing?

HAPPY TRAILS

Making a jolly rainbow is as easy as stacking colorful plates. Build in plates with clips so you can attach the rainbow to the bar at the back of the car.

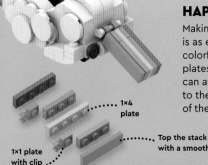

1×4 plate

Top the stack with a smooth tile

1×1 plate with clip

FLYING BOAT

Why not build a boat that can float through the sky as well as the water? With a propeller, wings, and a dash of magic, let your minifigures (and your imagination) soar. Use gold pieces, such as these wings, for a truly enchanted look.

It looks a bit cloudy over there...

Gold bar with side studs looks like a steering mechanism

Both wings connect to LEGO® Technic axles

If you don't have a rowboat piece, build your own

Propeller

Bar

Plate with clip

SET THE BAR HIGH

The boat's propeller slides onto a bar, which is held in place by a plate with clip.

Grab your bricks and make space to build.

CHAPTER 4
SPACE

CLASSIC ROCKET

Building space vehicles isn't rocket science! This ship is made mostly by stacking pieces from the bottom up. Build the body of the ship before connecting the engine below.

This mini stack makes a command module

BUILD TIP!

Use your widest pieces at the base and your narrowest pieces on top for a rocket shape.

When it comes to building, you can rock it!

4×4 round bricks make up the wide part of this ship

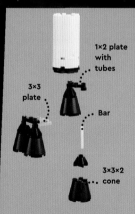

1×2 plate with tubes

3×3 plate

Bar

3×3×2 cone

SPACE BASE

Build each engine cone. Then attach them to a 3×3 plate so the engine can be joined securely to the rest of the rocket.

SELF-DRIVING ROCKET

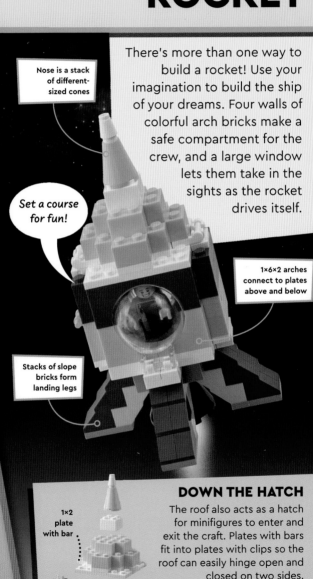

Nose is a stack of different-sized cones

There's more than one way to build a rocket! Use your imagination to build the ship of your dreams. Four walls of colorful arch bricks make a safe compartment for the crew, and a large window lets them take in the sights as the rocket drives itself.

Set a course for fun!

1×6×2 arches connect to plates above and below

Stacks of slope bricks form landing legs

DOWN THE HATCH

The roof also acts as a hatch for minifigures to enter and exit the craft. Plates with bars fit into plates with clips so the roof can easily hinge open and closed on two sides.

1×2 plate with bar

Two 1×1 plates with clips

COMMAND MODULE

The command module of this rocket is made from a 6×10 cylinder with open sides. Make a whole rocket by connecting the module to other parts of the craft using plates, or build the command module on its own.

I'm over the moon about this build!

Round plates join the different parts of this rocket ship

Bars fit into clips to make hatch handles

The roof is a 6×8 half cylinder with holes

Joystick

Minifigure attaches to the bottom of the cylinder

IN COMMAND

Add plenty of high-tech pieces inside, including joysticks for steering and lots of printed tiles for control panels.

BUILD TIP!

Add tiles with pin connectors to the round plates to make the connection between the module and other rocket parts more secure.

LANDING CAPSULE

Minifigure explorers need a craft like this one that lets them land on extraterrestrial surfaces. The tiles with clips act as landing legs when the door is open. They flip up to keep the hatch extra secure when the capsule is in flight mode.

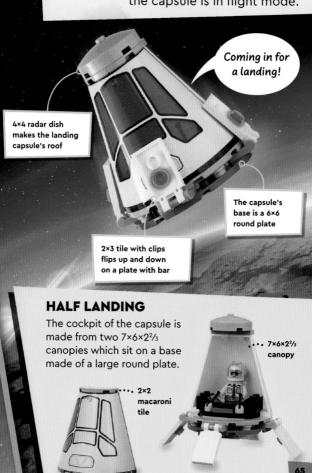

Coming in for a landing!

4×4 radar dish makes the landing capsule's roof

The capsule's base is a 6×6 round plate

2×3 tile with clips flips up and down on a plate with bar

HALF LANDING

The cockpit of the capsule is made from two 7×6×2⅔ canopies which sit on a base made of a large round plate.

7×6×2⅔ canopy

2×2 macaroni tile

ORBITING SHIP

What goes up must come down, so build a vehicle with a descent capsule to take your Earth-orbiting crew back to Earth. The round descent capsule on this ship can be removed to send minifigures home.

Hey, wait for me!

Connect the descent capsule to a 2×2 round plate

T-pieces look like communication antennas

LEGO® Technic ball and a round plate form the descent capsule

2×2 round plate with octagonal bar

2×2×2 robot body with axle hole

LEGO Technic axle

STAY CONNECTED

A LEGO Technic axle fits through two pieces with axle holes to securely connect both halves of the ship.

SPACE STATION

Minifigures who want to live and work among the stars need a sturdy space station. Use half cylinder pieces to form the crew's quarters and science lab. Pieces with clips and bars make the spacecraft's arms.

1×2 plate with clips fits onto a plate with bar

Two 2×4×5 half cylinders are held together by macaroni plates

BUILD TIP!

To stop the arms from snapping off, clip them to the space station once you've built the rest of the model.

Connect docking ships to this 2×2 truncated cone

Row of 1×2 transparent tiles

BRIGHT IDEA

The space station gets its electrical power from solar panels. Use dark transparent tiles to make your own energy collecting panels.

Tiles connect to plates below

PLANET EXPLORER

Make a small spacecraft for zipping around known and unknown planets across the universe. Leave room for a minifigure to take the controls and be sure your ship has plenty of power to move from place to place.

Two tiles with clips hold the large cockpit windshield

Where to next?

1×6 plates for extraterrestrial landing skids

MOVE ALONG

Two large engine pieces with 10 blades rotate inside LEGO® Technic cylinders to push this planet-exploring vehicle forward.

LEGO Technic cylinder

Large engine with 10 blades

SPACE MECH SUIT

A mechanical suit like this one lets minifigures safely explore all kinds of unfamiliar terrain on their expeditions. Use ball and socket joints or click hinge pieces so you can pose the legs and arms of your space mech suit.

This vehicle really suits me!

1×1 transparent cone makes a high-tech metal detector

1×2 plate with ball joint fits into a 1×2 plate with socket

Sturdy feet are sideways-built stacks

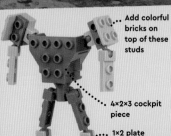

Add colorful bricks on top of these studs

4×2×3 cockpit piece

1×2 plate with socket

INSIDE OUT

Build the "skeleton" of the suit, including the cockpit, arms, and legs, before adding details and decorations.

SPACE SHUTTLE

These special space planes are reusable, and you can play with your shuttle again and again! Stick to your original design or add or swap out different colors and features.

BUILD TIP!

If you don't have hinge pieces, use standard bricks instead. Remove slopes as needed to open the bay doors.

How's it looking out there?

OPEN SPACE

Two rows of slope bricks fit onto long plates. These sit across two rows of hinge plates and bricks so that the cargo bay door can really open.

2×2 curved slope ......

1×8 plate ....

1×2 hinge brick and hinge plate ....

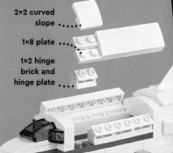

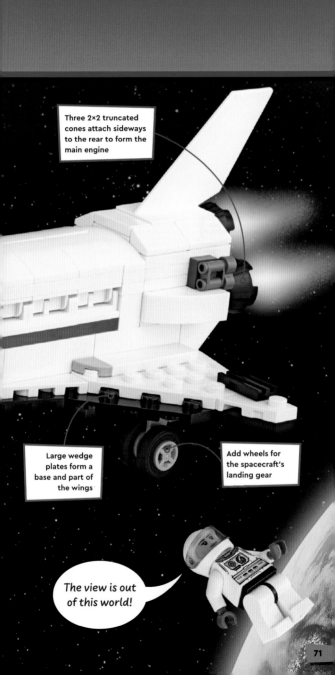

Three 2×2 truncated cones attach sideways to the rear to form the main engine

Large wedge plates form a base and part of the wings

Add wheels for the spacecraft's landing gear

The view is out of this world!

LUNAR LANDER

Even with moon-sized goals, you can make a realistic-looking model like this one with only a handful of bricks. Create an instantly recognizable lander by focusing on the details, such as these golden legs. They look just like the real thing.

1×1 round tile is the module's entry hatch

I think we left the manual on Earth!

Use gold pieces to look like the foil on the real lander

Plate and bar connections for poseable legs

ONE SMALL BRICK

Each part of this model attaches to one 1×1 brick with four side studs at the center.

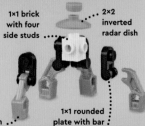

1×1 brick with four side studs ....

2×2 inverted radar dish

Robot arm ..•

1×1 rounded plate with bar :

SPEEDY SPACESHIP

Build a streamlined spaceship that can soar through starry skies. The spacecraft's curved slope nose and wedge plate wings make it aerodynamic. This means that air flows around the spaceship without slowing it down.

Streamlined nose is a 2×2 curved slope with lip

Transparent flame pieces for an extra-speedy look

You can't keep up with me!

Two 6×6 wedge plates make aerodynamic wings

HIDDEN TREASURE

Build a container box with a door into the back of the ship so your explorers can store all kinds of treasure from their travels.

1×1 rock crystal fits inside the container box

TIME MACHINE

Do your minifigures want to travel through space *and* time? Then you need to build a time machine. Build a sturdy vehicle on one large plate or two smaller plates like the two used in this model.

Transparent 1×1 round bricks represent time and space

I hope I arrive on time!

Four 2×2×3 corner slopes support the walls

Two 4×8 plates form the base of the time machine

Roof is a 6×6 plate

Stack of two 1×2 transparent bricks

OVERHEAD

Twelve 1×2 transparent bricks make windows and raise the height of the roof so that the minifigure can stand comfortably inside.

SPACE RACERS

The wings of each micro space racer look different, but they have one thing in common: they are all connected by clip and bar connections. Design yours however you like, then find out which is the fastest on the spacetrack!

I'm gaining on you!

The wing of this ship sits on a 1×2 plate with handle

Wedge plate wings can move up and down

1×2 plate with ball joint

1×2 plate with socket

1×4 plate covers the joint pieces

RACETRACK

Add obstacles to your course with hoops like this one. Ball and socket joints let the hoop curve into a circular shape.

Curved slopes give these wings their shape

ROCKET CAR

Minifigures will love driving a rocket car around town and blasting off to space whenever they like. This model is covered in smooth pieces for a sleek, high-tech look.

BUILD TIP!

Build the fins by stacking slope pieces. Then turn each fin on its side to connect it to the rocket car's sides.

The only visible studs are for the minifigure driver to connect to

Two 1×1 transparent slopes for a windshield

2×2×2 cone gives the rocket its iconic nose shape

Should I drive to the park or the moon?

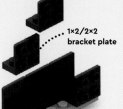

1×2/2×2 bracket plate

CELESTIAL BODY

This vehicle's body is a 2×6 plate with a row of 1×2/2×2 bracket plates on each side so that the rocket's fins can be attached.

2×6 plate

MOON BUGGY

Chunky tires are essential for a moon-roving vehicle like this one. Be sure to build in mudguards to keep the dust off the buggy and scientific equipment as your minifigures drive around, learning all about the moons they find.

Add an antenna to beam discoveries back to Earth

I wonder where the nearest garage is . . .

Build in a steering wheel so your explorer can drive

Tires fit onto 2×2 plates with wheel-holding pins

COOL TOOLS

1×1 plate with bar

Antenna connects to jumper plate below

Build research equipment for your buggy with just a few small pieces. Inverted dishes could be satellites or special detectors.

2×2 inverted dish

BRICK TYPES

When you're planning your vehicle models, it can be helpful to know which LEGO® pieces you have and what they are called. These are just some of the many LEGO parts you may come across. If you don't have all of these pieces, don't worry! You can make lots of impressive models with the elements you do have.

What brick will I pick?

⚠ Small parts and small balls can cause choking if swallowed. Not for children under 3 years.

MEASUREMENTS

The size of a LEGO piece is described by the number of studs it has. A brick that has two studs along and three studs up is called a 2×3 brick. Tall parts have a third number, which is the height of the piece in standard bricks.

2×3 brick top view

2×3 brick side view

1×1×3 brick side view

BRICKS

Bricks are the basis of most builds. They come in many shapes, sizes, and colors.

2×2 brick

2×2 round brick

1×2 brick

PLATES

Plates have studs on top and tubes on the bottom, but plates are thinner than bricks. Three stacked plates are the same height as one standard brick.

=

3 stacked 1×2 plates next to a 1×2 brick

2×3 plate

1×1 plate

JUMPER PLATES

These plates have just one stud in the middle, and they let you "jump" the usual grid of LEGO studs. These pieces are useful for centering things in your models.

2×2 jumper plate

1×2 jumper plate

TILES

Tiles have tubes on the bottom and no studs on top. These parts give your builds a smooth finish, and printed tiles add more detail.

2×2 tile

Printed eye tile

SIDE STUDS

Pieces with studs on more than one side let you build upward as well as outward.

1×1 brick with side stud

1×2/2×2 bracket

CLIPS

Pieces with clips can attach to other elements, such as bars.

1×2 plate with two clips

1×1 plate with clip

LEGO® TECHNIC

These elements expand the range of functions you can build into your models. They are particularly useful for builds with lots of moving parts or technical details.

1×2 brick with axle hole

LEGO® Technic axle

JOINTS

Add flexibility to your build with parts that have tow balls and sockets.

1×2 plate with ball socket

1×2 plate with tow ball

SLOPES

Slope bricks have diagonal angles. They can be curved or inverted (upside down).

1×1 slope

2×1 inverted slope

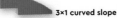

3×1 curved slope

HINGES

Add movement to your builds with hinge pieces. Hinge plates and hinge bricks let parts of your builds move from side to side or tilt up and down.

1×2 hinge brick with 2×2 hinge plate (side view)

1×2 hinge brick with 2×2 hinge plate (top view)

DK | Penguin Random House

Senior Editor Tori Kosara
Designers James McKeag and Isabelle Merry
Production Editor Siu Yin Chan
Senior Production Controller Lloyd Robertson
Managing Editor Paula Regan
Managing Art Editor Jo Connor
Publishing Director Mark Searle

Inspirational models built by
Mariann Asanuma, Jason Briscoe, Emily Corl, Nate Dias,
Jessica Farrell, Rod Gillies, Tim Goddard, Kevin Hall, Barney Main,
Simon Pickard, and Iain Scott

Photography by Gary Ombler

Cover design by James McKeag

Dorling Kindersley would like to thank:
Randi Sørensen, Heidi K. Jensen, Lydia Barram, Ashley Blais,
Paul Hansford, Martin Leighton Lindhart, Martin Klingenberg,
Nina Koopman, and the LEGO City Design Team at the LEGO Group;
Julia March for proofreading; and Kayla Dugger for Americanization.

First American Edition, 2023
Published in the United States by DK Publishing
1745 Broadway, 20th Floor, New York, NY 10019

Page design copyright © 2023 Dorling Kindersley Limited
DK, a Division of Penguin Random House LLC
23 24 25 26 27 10 9 8 7 6 5 4 3 2
002–333940–Mar/2023

LEGO, the LEGO logo, the Minifigure, and the
Brick and Knob configurations are trademarks
and/or copyrights of the LEGO Group.
©2023 The LEGO Group. All rights reserved.

Manufactured by Dorling Kindersley,
One Embassy Gardens, 8 Viaduct Gardens, London SW11 7BW, UK
under license from the LEGO Group.

Contains content previously published in How to Build LEGO® Cars (2021), LEGO®
Amazing Vehicles (2019), LEGO® City Build Your Own Adventure: Catch the
Crooks (2020), LEGO® Epic History (2020), LEGO® Halloween Ideas (2020), LEGO®
Magical Ideas (2021), LEGO® Minifigure Mission (2021), and
The LEGO® Ideas Book (2022)

A catalog record for this book
is available from the Library of Congress.
ISBN 978-0-7440-7653-0
Printed and bound in China

For the curious

www.dk.com
www.LEGO.com

MIX
Paper | Supporting
responsible forestry
FSC™ C018179

This book was made with Forest
Stewardship Council ™ certified
paper–one small step in DK's
commitment to a sustainable future.
For more information go to
www.dk.com/our-green-pledge